Creating a Professional Development School

by
Nancy Bacharach
and
Robin Hasslen

D1713076

ISBN 0-87367-680-7
Copyright © 2001 by the Phi Delta Kappa Educational Foundation
Bloomington, Indiana

This fastback is sponsored by the
Sinnissippi Illinois Chapter
of Phi Delta Kappa International,
which made a generous contribution
toward publication costs.

Table of Contents

Professional Development Schools

Our schools face increasing challenges, and institutions that prepare teachers are being forced to re-examine curricula and programs. Teacher educators must prepare teachers who are responsible for meeting the diverse needs of 21st century students. One of the most promising efforts for addressing these increasing challenges is the professional development school. A PDS is a functioning public school where school and university personnel work collaboratively to create an exemplary learning environment that is capable of transforming both teacher preparation and the schooling of children from pre-K through grade 12 (Million and Vare 1997).

A Working Definition

Public schools and universities have each taken on a separate and distinct role in preparing teachers. University faculty typically teach the foundation and theories of learning, along with various teaching methods. Public schools provide the "hands-on" practice where prospective teachers try out their skills in working with students. Although university faculty have typically supervised these prospective teachers, the relationships between faculty and public school teachers have been limited. However, in a professional development school, university faculty and school-based personnel *collaboratively* reshape both the teacher education program and the curriculum and instruction for pre-K-12 students. One teacher in a PDS stated:

> On the one hand, teachers have been exposed to the newest teaching techniques and information through the involvement of the university faculty. On the other hand, we have had the opportunity for major input into the content and delivery of a realistic teacher training program.

The term *professional development school* has been attached to a variety of collaborative efforts. These projects range from university personnel supervising a small group of preservice teachers at a school site to what Goodlad calls a *symbiotic partnership*, where "school and university personnel share the decisions of operating both the school and the entire length and breadth of the teacher education program" (Sirotnik and Goodlad 1988, p. 85). While models and definitions abound, Teitel offers the following definition: "PDSs are collaborations between schools and colleges focusing on high-quality education for diverse students, the preparation of preservice educators, and continuous inquiry into improving practice. The intention of this collaboration is to connect theory and practice in education so they reciprocally inform each other" (1998*b*, p. 85).

A Brief History

The idea of school-university collaboration is not new. Almost a century ago John Dewey urged the new schools of education to examine the preparation of doctors and lawyers to "learn from the more intensive and matured experience of other callings" (Dewey 1904/1974, p. 10). Dewey believed that teachers needed a certain amount of practical work along with the theoretical. While Dewey's vision remains largely unfulfilled, the education community appears to be reexamining and embracing Dewey's premise entering the 21st century.

The emergence of school-university partnerships has been driven by two major reports. The Carnegie Forum on Education and the Economy (1986) supported *clinical schools*, where public schools worked collaboratively with colleges of education and university arts and sciences faculty to prepare future teachers. The Holmes Group recommended the establishment of *professional development schools*. They believed the PDS "would provide superior opportunities for teachers and administrators to influence the development of their profession, and for university faculty to increase the professional relevance of their work" (1986, p. 56). Similar school-university partnerships were also suggested by Goodlad (1984), the Ford Foundation (Anderson 1993), and the RAND Corporation (Wise and Darling-Hammond 1987).

Each of these prominent groups focused on the need for schools and universities to work together to bring about change in both public schools and university teacher preparation programs. Several authors compared the PDS to the teaching hospital in medicine. Like teaching hospitals, PDS provide real-life, supervised experiences through which prospective teachers have the opportunity first to observe, then to assist, and eventually to solo in their journey to becoming certified teachers.

As late as 1992, Abdal-Haqq could find no fully developed PDS. Since then, there has been an explosion in their number. While it is hard to know how many PDS really exist, data from the last decade indicate that 46% of the nation's teacher education programs are aligned with more than 1,000 individual professional development schools (Abdal-Haqq 1998*b*). PDS are found in 47 states in urban, suburban, and rural areas and include elementary, middle, and high schools. This increase is dramatic, and the numbers appear to be growing.

Benefits, Barriers, and Goals

The decision to participate in a PDS is not one to be taken lightly. It is important for participants to examine both the benefits and the barriers to such an endeavor.

Benefits

A PDS provides opportunities for teachers at both the school and university to share information and ideas. Each can learn something new. The opportunity to discuss education issues is a valuable gift. Teachers today face staggering workloads and have little time for professional reflection and growth. PDS offer teachers a unique opportunity to "step back from their classrooms and reflect on teaching and the broader profession" (Auton and Futrell 1998, p. 3).

A PDS also offers public school teachers the chance to participate as partners in education research. Teachers work together with university faculty to study instructional strategies and curricula for students and preservice teachers. University faculty also have an opportunity to participate and learn about the realities of today's classrooms. One university faculty member commented:

> While I have had constant connections with classrooms in the past, this year I was not only the university supervisor, I was a member of the school community. I spent lots of time in classrooms observing, assessing, assisting, and actually teaching. I feel I have a better and more realistic view of what it takes to be a teacher today.

Having additional adults in the public schools also is beneficial. One teacher noted:

> Young children have had more adults with various talents and energy levels to learn from and interact with. They have been able to have significant attention from adults who care.

Barriers

The Holmes Group (1995) warns that the creation of a PDS is a difficult undertaking. It is important to identify and be ready for the challenges that typically arise during the development of a new partnership. One of the first major hurdles to overcome is the creation of a shared vision. Teacher educators traditionally are focused on theory, while classroom teachers are immersed in practice. These different foci result in the creation of different goals. For example, teachers in a PDS tend to focus on the perceived benefits of having additional pairs of hands to help out in the classroom. University faculty, on the other hand, put their focus on the preparation of preservice teachers. Creating a shared vision means that the two groups must identify and jointly assume responsibility for all learners in the school, whether that learner is a second-grader, a preservice teacher, a cooperating teacher, or a university faculty member.

A second major barrier lies in the two very different cultures of the institutions. Work tempo, work focus, rewards, and degrees of power and autonomy differ dramatically between universities and public schools (Brookhart and Loadman 1990). It is imperative that both teachers and faculty members recognize and understand the differences in these cultures and come to terms with these differences.

Another challenge for the PDS is defining the roles and responsibilities of each of the participants. Understanding what is expected of each person helps to alleviate the hard feelings that can arise when someone is not doing what others expect him or her to do. An additional critical factor for successful collaboration is time (Hoerr 1997). Newcomers to collaboration often are unaware of the amount of time necessary to meet with others, to come to consensus about their work, and to do so on a regular basis. Possibly the most important challenge is for the group to engage in ongoing, open, and honest communication. This helps to overcome cultural differences, to build trust, and to create a common vision. Darling-Hammond urges participants to look on information as a "cherished commodity that should be widely shared" (1994, p. 216). One teacher stated the need eloquently:

Finding people who can really work at understanding each institution's culture, goals, and needs is paramount. We need to put personal agendas aside and become people who truly know what compromise and collaboration is all about. We need people who are listeners and thinkers, respectful of others' needs and empathetic in actions and words.

Setting Goals

The goals for professional development schools are diverse. Each partnership creates objectives that are specific to their site. However, every PDS should have, at its core, four main goals, which are to provide:

- exemplary education for pre-K-12 student development and learning;
- preservice education for new teachers and other school personnel;
- professional development for teachers and faculty; and
- applied study of practice designed to improve instruction.

In a PDS, prospective and novice teachers learn from and work alongside veteran teachers while the veterans simultaneously engage in their own professional development. The PDS supports teachers and faculty in collaboratively studying their own practice. A teacher in a PDS spoke about the collaboration, saying,

Having the opportunity to discuss issues with other professionals — teachers and university faculty — was very powerful. The interactions with college faculty on an almost daily basis enrich my professional growth. I feel like I have grown so much over the year and that my students are the direct beneficiaries of our collaborative efforts.

As professional development schools go about their work, the focus should be on the inclusion of the best available knowledge in teaching and learning, which ultimately should lead to the renewal of both the schools and teacher education. The current model of teacher education and reform in pre-K-12 classrooms has long been disjointed. Professional development schools allow for integration of resources and a focus on the core practices of teaching and learning (Clark 1997).

Integrating the Goals with PDS Standards

In an effort to help define and institutionalize the PDS, the National Council for Accreditation of Teacher Education (1997) developed a set of standards for identifying and supporting high-quality professional development schools. The purposes of the standards are to identify the important characteristics of a PDS and to delineate the critical attributes necessary for a successful collaboration. The standards recognize three stages of PDS development that partners will go through, including pre-threshold, threshold, and quality attainment. In the pre-threshold phase, partners build relationships and trust through collaborative ventures. This stage often is characterized by individual relationships, and it tends to lack the institutional commitment necessary for widespread support. In the threshold stage, a formal agreement committing the school and the university to the basic goals of the PDS is adopted. The third stage, quality attainment, incorporates a list of essential attributes and evidence of their achievement in fulfilling the PDS mission. These critical attributes include:

- *Learning theory*: The PDS is a learning-centered community characterized by norms and practices that support adult and children's learning.
- *Collaboration*: The PDS is characterized by joint work between and among school and university faculty directed at implementing the mission.
- *Accountability and quality assurance*: The PDS is accountable to the public and to the profession for upholding professional standards for teaching and learning and for preparing new teachers in accordance with these standards.
- *Organization, roles, and structures*: The PDS uses processes and allocates resources and time to systematize the continuous improvement of learning to teach, teaching, learning, and organizational life.
- *Equity*: A PDS is characterized by norms and practices that support equity and learning by all students and adults (NCATE 1997).

The standards provide indicators and examples for each condition of the threshold phase and for each essential attribute in the quality attainment phase. These guidelines should be required reading for any group considering the establishment of a PDS.

How to Establish a PDS

In developing a PDS, it is useful to frame sets of questions around key issues. The first of these issues is assessing current practices in the school and the university that seek to form a partnership.

Assessing Institutional Practices

What is the history of collaboration between the institutions?

Education institutions planning to establish partnerships must first assess the history that has existed between them. How invested are the partners beyond a few individuals or administrators? What degree of collaboration already has occurred, in what types of arenas, and with how many partners involved? What perceptions are held by each group about the other's culture? What events or interactions may have occurred to taint the relationships or to cause ill will among some of the members of the institutions?

The values of working together versus alone, of providing and receiving assistance versus being self-contained, are essential cultural attributes about which potential partners need to be aware. Darling-Hammond warns those undertaking such partnerships that "PDSs are especially challenging collaborations because they seek to reshape fundamental values, beliefs, and paradigms for schools and school change while they are negotiating two worlds and inventing new programs" (1994, p. 21).

Who are the participants?

While the participants in a school/university partnership share the goal of providing a high-quality education, their methods for providing that education often are at odds as individuals and institutions guard their turf. Despite the numerous and changing participants at varying levels in the partnership, it is essential that those in leadership remain strongly supportive of the concept.

It usually is unwise to assign educators roles in a collaborative venture. Despite their commitments to the field of education, they are not always interested in collaborating nor do they always possess the necessary skills for working together. In a successful PDS, the individuals involved are usually people who choose to participate, are interested in education reform and professional development, and are open to working together.

For the university, it is useful to include university faculty from departments other than education, such as the arts and sciences and other disciplines. Doing so broadens the scope of the PDS and provides greater resources for the school and the university. Similarly, it is important for the public schools to involve auxiliary personnel in addition to classroom teachers. Community members also should be involved and can be employed as mentors, tutors, and so on. In this way, the community gains ownership in the school and develops a deeper understanding of current education practices.

Finally, it is important to involve an outside evaluator who can provide an objective analysis of activities and progress. This is important to the integrity of the partnership, especially when disputes arise.

What are the common needs and goals?

Don't be afraid to ask all the potential participants from the outset, "What do you want to gain from this partnership?" A true partnership is different from many cooperative ventures in that it is a relationship whose needs and goals cannot be met and accomplished alone. When all the participants agree on a set of goals for the partnership, the individual participants can come and go without threatening the demise of the partnership.

Faculty may find that outside of such a goal their work often goes unnoticed and without reward. They also may be isolated and lack professional support. Apart from this larger vision of renewal, educators at times may become confused about education practices and goals (Lieberman and Miller 1984). In addition, holding teachers accountable for improved learning without some assistance is difficult, according to Goodlad (1984), who with Lipsky (1980) argues for the meshing of school improvement, staff development, and collaborative efforts.

Goals must be shared, but they can vary from one PDS to another. However, one common goal for all involved in the collaborative effort is education renewal.

What can institutions offer each other?

Traditionally, colleges and universities have provided the theoretical framework for education practice while the schools have served as the place of practice. In a PDS, the roles are intertwined and equitable. Classroom teachers are partners in developing and delivering the preservice teacher curriculum. University faculty members and public school teachers work side by side in studying best practice. Every participant becomes both a teacher and a learner at various times.

Schools and universities complement each other. Hathaway explains: "The university and the school district are each other's own best resources. Between them, school districts and universities cover virtually the whole range of human learning. That we are interconnected is undeniable. The challenge before us is to realize and build upon the extent, the possibilities, and the necessity of our connection and dependence" (1985, p. 4).

Gaining Support from the Institutions

How will the partnership be funded?

Funding needs to be considered carefully at the outset so that partnerships are not formed and later dissolved because of a lack of funds. It has been estimated that, on average, $50,000 will suffice to cover start-up costs for a 2-year development project between two sites (Clark 1997).

In many cases, a PDS will acquire funds from joint commitments by the university and the school district.

In some locations, universities have reallocated funds from programs that the PDS displaces. A third option is external funding. However, with external funding, the participants in the PDS need to be assured that initial funding will provide adequate time for planning, developing, and establishing a PDS. When funding has to be sought annually, it is stressful and time-consuming and detracts from more important goals of the PDS. Often institutions receive start-up funds for a PDS and manage to get the first year or two going with a flourish of supported activity. However, when funding sources dry up or people are unable to secure additional or in-house monies, the projects often end.

In addition to the concern about adequacy of funds, there need to be safeguards in place for administering the funds. It is important to ensure that funds are administered by all institutions in the partnership, rather than controlled by just one of the agencies.

Developing the Initial Idea

What is needed to plan for the partnership?

Goodlad reiterates, "The right beginning is critical" (1994, p. 105). Thus there must be adequate *planning time* before the partnership is initiated. In addition, all the participants must be part of that planning; administrators cannot simply decree that a PDS will be established. It might be necessary to devote a year or two for planning. Time also is needed to establish a sense of trust and ease in communication among the partners (Bell 1995).

Communication is an ongoing concern and an absolute necessity for the success of a collaborative venture. It is important for communication to occur among all the participants. Unfortunately, it often is neglected beyond the "inner circle." This creates misperceptions, jealousies, and a lack of shared visions. The wider the area of communication and the more frequently it occurs, the more successful the partnership will be.

Another important initial step in establishing a PDS is to *define roles and responsibilities* (Miller and Silvernail 1994; Sandholtz and Finan 1998). There should be two site coordinators, one a school teacher and the other a university faculty member. These coordinators have responsibility for a variety of activities, such as arranging placements for interns and cooperating teachers, advising and supervising interns, supporting professional development, providing resources, modeling lessons, co-teaching, arranging community and parent involvement, solving problems on a daily basis, and being a visible presence in the school building. Once these individuals are in place, there can be additional definition of responsibilities for other participants.

In addition, equitable *inter-institutional authority and fiscal responsibility* must be established at the start if the partnership is to succeed (Neufeld 1992). When one institution holds too much of the power or purse strings, hard feelings can arise. Appointing co-directors or calling on administrators already in place to carry out these responsibilities are two means of alleviating problems of authority. As often as possible, all participants should be apprised of the budget allocations and accounts.

While it may seem insignificant in light of issues of participants and funding, the need for *physical space* within the school facilities also is of great importance. An adequate location provides the PDS with a presence in the building. It serves as a place for sharing information. For community members and parents who might be volunteering in the school, the PDS office can be a welcoming area. Psychologically, a specific space provides an important identity and establishes some stability and credibility for the partnership.

Finally, it is important that institutions establish a *written commitment* to the partnership. The agreement should commit all of the partners to the basic mission of the PDS. Lee Teitel (1998a) has provided some examples of sample agreements and a "tool kit" for examining governance structures. This information is helpful for starting, as well as sustaining, professional development schools.

Finding Interested Participants

Which university and school district personnel should participate?

It is important to allow participants to volunteer for participation, rather than to be forced into the partnership. Educators who agree to participate in a PDS have often volunteered for various new initiatives. They usually are risk-takers and innovators.

However, it also is important that a PDS become a "whole school" project, rather than a "school-within-a-school," which can lead to negative divisions and misperceptions. To establish this type of entire-school involvement, teachers should be able to choose their level of involvement. The Learning Connections Laboratory in St. Cloud, Minnesota, developed a model to describe the possible levels of involvement:

Level 1, Collaborating Teacher: Willing to serve as co-operating teacher for an intern for the entire school year and be involved in weekly professional development sessions.

Level 2, Cooperating Teacher: Willing to serve as cooperating teacher for an intern for the entire school year, but *not* be involved in weekly professional development sessions.

Level 3, Contributing Teacher: Willing to serve as cooperating teacher in various capacities, *not* on a full-year, full-time basis and *not* involved in weekly PDS meetings.

Level 4, Supporting Teacher: Willing to support the PDS in smaller, more specific ways, such as teaching a session for the interns, doing a demonstration classroom activity, etc.

At the end of each school year, teachers are provided the opportunity to select their level of involvement for the following year.

University faculty should have similar opportunities for participation within a PDS. Unfortunately, because of the reward structure at many institutions, there is little incentive for university faculty to be involved in a PDS. Senior faculty often are involved in research that affords them little time to devote to interactions within the public schools; and junior faculty must be careful to fulfill necessary criteria for tenure and advancement, which often focus on research and publishing, not school-university collaboration. However, institutions of higher education are beginning to see the importance of collaborative ventures and are coming to recognize faculty efforts in such partnerships. Universities with more progressive colleges of education and deans have recognized PDS involvement as not merely service, but as venues for valid research and education renewal; and they have rewarded faculty accordingly.

There also are few incentives for public school teachers to become involved in a PDS (Sandholtz and Merseth 1992; Sandholtz and Finan 1998). Successful professional development schools have been innovative in creating reward structures and have provided such incentives as salary changes, college credits, recognition, and professional development opportunities (for example, funding conference or workshop attendance).

What skills should participants possess?

It has been suggested by some (Peterson 1977; Sarason et al. 1977) that successful partnerships rely, at least initially, on a persistent, dynamic individual whose ideas and innovations inspire the collaboration of others. Such charismatic leaders often are at the forefront of many new initiatives. However, to rely solely for any length of time on such an individual can be detrimental to the longevity of the partnership.

A diversity of skills and experiences are needed. However, all partners must have an ability to understand

and move between the cultures of the institutions involved. Individuals involved in a PDS should be able to share responsibilities for administering and coordinating all aspects of the project. They must demonstrate a commitment to improving teacher education and professional growth, to collaboration and teaming, and to the continuing examination of teaching and best practice.

The PDS participants need to be risk-takers, individuals who are willing to "think outside the box," who will try and try again, who can accept critiques, who can go to bed frustrated and awake with renewed vigor, and who maintain a sense of humor.

Creating a Shared Vision

Why should participants create a shared vision for the PDS?

Absence of a shared vision dooms a PDS to failure. Unfortunately, participants often begin by articulating a shared vision and then subscribe to different views and goals.

It is essential that the vision be truly "shared," having grown out of discussions involving all parties. It must be inclusive and envelop the concerns of both institutions and all participants. It should be concise and clearly articulated so that everyone understands the purpose of the collaboration.

It will take time to create a shared vision. For example, in one PDS the public school teachers were focused solely on developing new curricula, while the university faculty were intent on gathering data about the effect of the PDS on preservice teachers. It took an entire school year for both partners to broaden their perspectives to be able to envision and incorporate the overarching goal of the project into their thinking and activities.

Getting to Know One Another

Can differences between school cultures be overcome?

First of all, recognition of the existence of different cultures is necessary and healthy. Without attempting to assimilate each other, it is important that partners use each other's strengths and skills and understand when differences erect barriers to progress. Haberman (1971) has offered an interesting picture of the two groups:

> Public school people regard college people as too theoretical and more concerned with analysis than solutions, not capable of working within legal structures, incapable of hard work during regularly scheduled business hours. College people perceive public school people as too conservative in accepting research or responding to great social problems; fearful of superiors; of lower intelligence, status, and education. (p. 134)

These two portraits of the participants must be dismantled and discussed by all the participants in the project. It is important for school personnel, for instance, to understand that in addition to teaching responsibilities, university faculty are required to serve on numerous committees; advise undergraduate and graduate students; design, conduct, analyze, and disseminate research; and provide university and community service. University faculty, on the other hand, need to understand and appreciate the constant demands that teachers face daily in their classrooms.

How are relationships formed to establish trust?

Partnerships are best built on an existing foundation of positive relationships developed through student teaching or practicum placements and the inherent responsibilities of teachers and faculty. In those cases, a certain amount of trust and respect already has developed. However, it is important not to assume that such relationships will sustain the more intense partnership of a PDS.

All participants must spend the time to get to know one another on personal and professional levels. Icebreaker activities, social gatherings, and focused discussions are necessary not only as a partnership begins, but also as the partnership matures and new participants join the group. In one PDS, because prior relationships existed between the schools and the university, it was assumed that the participants could get down to business without worrying about building trust. Unfortunately, as issues began to surface, institutional cultures dominated discussions and cloaked perceptions and misperceptions stood in the way of objectively solving problems. Fortunately, the group was able to stop midstream and concentrate on team-building. However, a good deal of the pain and misunderstanding could not be erased by then.

Determining Who Decides What and How

Are there power issues to be addressed?

The concept of power often is perceived negatively and with great suspicion. In a collaborative venture, power is necessary; but it must be shared so that owner-ship and leadership are experienced by all participants. A partnership built around a powerful individual or group is certain to fail unless that individual or group begins to empower others by providing them with re-sponsibilities and leadership. Discussion of who makes what types of decisions is an important first step in set-ting up the partnership.

Who makes the decisions about what issues?
Sometimes the participants in a PDS try to make de-cisions by consensus at every level and for every issue. However ideal such a process appears, it is often too time-consuming and assumes a lack of trust in the roles and responsibilities of all the participants.

A helpful exercise early in the planning stages of a partnership might involve large-group discussions about who should be responsible for which decisions. Some decisions can be made at the site level, some by an advisory board, some at an administrative level, and so forth. Having the process defined by consensus makes it easier to reach decisions later.

The fact that a partnership consists of equal partners does not preclude the need for a certain amount of structure. In every group, there should be representatives of both insti-tutions; and parents and community members should be involved as often as possible. A governing board should in-clude the top administrators (superintendents and deans), an executive director or co-directors in charge of manager-ial and leadership responsibilities, and institutional repre-sentatives. Some professional development schools include student interns on their boards. Committees or work groups should be formed to undertake specific tasks that are better accomplished by small groups.

Communication is a key ingredient for the success of collaborations structured with numerous governing and working bodies. When participants are assured of representation on boards and are kept abreast of decisions and activities, there is little concern about hidden agendas or lack of input. However, once again, the issue of trust arises. When participants are unable to trust others to make decisions that are in the best interest of all, then few decisions are made in a timely manner.

Assessing Progress

How important is ongoing assessment?

Evaluation is essential, and it must be continuous. The participants need to document the effect of the PDS on student learning, teacher preparation, and professional development.

Evaluations should be undertaken both internally and externally and should be both formative and summative. There are a number of challenges, however, in documenting the effect of a PDS. Teitel (1999, p. 5) believes the following areas of difficulty are evident:

- Establishing control groups.
- Differing perceptions of what outcomes are important.
- Differing ideas on how to measure outcomes.
- Possibility that it may be too early in the cycle of the innovation to evaluate it.

- Risk of jeopardizing fragile relationships by premature evaluation.
- Difficulty allocating time for documentation.

In addition to evaluating the collaborative work, there must be assessments of student achievement, an area that until recently was rarely addressed. However, teachers and school districts need to recognize that some changes in student achievement might not be evident in a year's time and that such assessment has to be longitudinal.

Partners often enthuse following a year of collaboration that they "feel good" about what they did. Such a statement, no matter how heartfelt, is insufficient to convince funding bodies or institutions to sustain collaborative ventures.

Who needs to be accountable?

Teachers, university faculty, administrators, interns — in short, all of the partners — are accountable for education renewal and student achievement. The importance of collecting data cannot be understated. And numerous assessment tools and measures are essential to paint a complete picture of a partnership. The exciting part of accountability in a PDS is that everyone is involved at various levels; responsibility and accountability go hand in hand but do not rest on individual accomplishments or failures.

How are results disseminated to a broader audience?

There are numerous ways to provide information to the public and to groups interested in the PDS. However, it should be remembered that such dissemination, whether in written or oral form, should be done collaboratively. As a reflection of a partnership, all voices should be part of what the rest of the world hears when reflections or evaluations of collaborations are disseminated.

Information should always be conveyed within the PDS itself. Beyond the school, it is essential that the district administrators and school board are kept informed. University faculty, both within and beyond the college of education, should be aware of the PDS, its process, and its outcomes. University administrators also should understand the importance of collaboration within the community. It is essential that both institutions perceive the PDS as more than a "lab school" for one or the other's benefit.

Furthermore, students, parents, and members of the larger community should be kept informed of PDS activities in order to continue to support PDS efforts. This kind of dissemination has been done very successfully through family nights and instructional evenings that are attended by university and school faculty, interns, families, and their children.

Efforts in education renewal need to extend further than the surrounding neighborhood and to include the larger research and education community across the country. Thus dissemination at regional, state, and national conferences and through journals is essential to broaden the knowledge base and learn from each other's successes and challenges. While such activity is customary for university faculty, it has been new and exciting for school teachers. They have reported a new sense of empowerment and professionalism following presentations and participation in state and national conferences.

Surviving the First Year

What issues are almost certain to arise early in a partnership?

Inherent in the PDS model are such issues as control, decision making, trust, communication, institutional barriers, philosophies of organizational change, reward systems, research and practice, individual and organizational interests, involvement of participants, selection of common issues, assessment, resources, problems with interpersonal attitudes and behaviors, and time.

How will those issues be addressed?

Time is a critical factor for developing initial ideas, building trust among the partners, reflecting on practice, guiding preservice teachers, and forging community relationships. Innovative methods of finding time have included: 1) freed-up time (use of others to teach; early release days), 2) restructured or rescheduled time (lengthen four or five days with early release on fifth day), 3) better use of time (using school meetings for professional development or PDS business), 4) common time (meshing schedules for planning), and 5) purchased time (establishing a substitute bank that teachers can use for PDS activities) (Watts and Castle 1993).

The PDS will require more on-site time by university faculty, who may not be released from their standard course loads. These faculty have found that clustering interns and teaching some courses on site provides them with some extra time (Hausfather, Outlaw, and Strehle 1996).

The lack of rewards for participants at both institutions continues to be a concern (Goodlad 1975; Lieberman 1986; Parkay 1986). In fact, some researchers have reported that the reward structures at colleges and universities are a primary barrier to working in a PDS (Button, Ponticell, and Johnson 1996). It is essential that deans, department chairs, and colleagues recognize the necessity of collaboration for continuous improvement of teacher preparation and the contribution it makes to the knowledge base for teacher education.

Looking Ahead

How is a PDS sustained when soft money disappears?

It is certainly exciting to develop a PDS with ample external funding, to start up with money for "extras" and for state-of-the-art technology. But it is difficult to acquire funding for maintaining ventures once the development stages are completed. That is especially true when the PDS is seen as an add-on to regular teacher preparation programs (Sykes 1997).

Clark (1997) found several approaches that successfully maintained PDS structures once the soft money gave out. Funds were redirected from other programs. Both institutions committed necessary operating costs. Groups became innovative in combining institutional support with external funding, frequently through smaller grants.

Why are participants eager to continue or weary of the work?

Partnerships can be time-consuming, tiring, and stressful. Teachers can suffer burnout when participation in the PDS equals overload. While creative solutions have been attempted to alleviate the time demands on the teachers (for example, continuing education credits, release time, professional development, program improvement, extra compensation), it has been difficult to determine the long-term effect of such solutions.

Teachers involved in one PDS gave this advice to teachers considering working in a partnership:

- Enter with enthusiasm and an open mind.
- Be aware of the time commitment.
- Value professional development time away from the classroom.
- Know the importance of creating better teachers.
- Maintain a positive outlook.
- Don't try to do too much at once.
- Be broad-minded.
- Be willing and able to communicate.
- Don't be afraid to have 20 people in your room.
- Be flexible.
- Desire to improve.
- Work toward consensus.
- Be a team player.

Numerous studies from PDS sites across the country discuss the benefits of being in a PDS. Some of these benefits include:

- Mutual professional development occurs for university and school personnel.
- More adults are available to students to help them in the classroom.
- University faculty gain insights into connections between theory and practice.
- Preservice teachers have longer, sustained experiences in schools.
- Preservice teachers prepared in a PDS tend to be more reflective, assume leadership roles more quickly, and are generally more successful novice teachers.
- Preservice teachers are instrumental in changing practices of mentor teachers.

Conclusion

It is imperative that we seek the best for children. To do that we must break down the barriers that currently exist between the worlds of theory and practice and between the university and the public school. Working collaboratively, the wisdom and experience of the participants has the potential to create new, exciting learning environments and practices that meet the needs of future generations of children.

Although teaching styles are changing, there are few opportunities for true collaboration in the field of education. Teachers and faculty teach alone. Thus the most rewarding outcomes for educators in a PDS are the personal networking and collegiality built across institutions (Bercik 1991). Teachers who formerly worked alone (and burned out alone) have experienced renewed energy and enthusiasm for teaching, have understood the essential nature of continued professional development, and have delighted in the contagious air of education renewal evident in their schools.

Designing, developing, and sustaining a professional development school is risky business. There are no exact blueprints to follow, no detours around inevitable problems, and no guarantees of success. However, there are almost certain to be successful outcomes for educators and students when goals are held in common, trust is established among the participants, and communication is open and ongoing.

As we continue to gather information about professional development schools, we are certain to find better ways to sustain partnerships; but we will be building on what we have learned thus far. And we will create the knowledge that informs and guides education renewal.

Resources

Abdal-Haqq, I. "Professional Development Schools and Educational Reform: Concepts and Concerns." *ERIC Digest* 91, no. 2 (1992): 1-4.

Abdal-Haqq, I. *Professional Development Schools: Weighing the Evidence*. Thousand Oaks, Calif.: Corwin, 1998. a

Abdal-Haqq, I. "Professional Development Schools: What Do We Know? What Do We Need to Know? How Do We Find Out? Who Do We Tell?" Paper presented at the National Professional Development School Conference, Baltimore, 16 October 1998. ERIC Document Reproduction Service No. ED425142. b

Anderson, C.R., ed. *Voices of Change: A Report of the Clinical Schools Project*. Washington, D.C.: American Association of Colleges for Teacher Education, 1993.

Auton, S., and Futrell, M. "The Road to Professionalization: A Challenge to ATE." *ATE Newsletter*. Reston, Va.: Association of Teacher Educators, November-December 1998.

Bell, N.M. *Professional Development Sites: Revitalizing Preservice Education in Middle Schools*. 1995. ERIC Document Reproduction Service No. ED382583.

Bercik, J.T. "University/District Apprenticeship Model Development." 1991. ERIC Document Reproduction Service No. ED378149.

Brookhart, S., and Loadman, W. "School-University Collaboration: Different Workplace Culture." *Contemporary Education* 61(Spring 1990): 125-28.

Bullough, R., et al. "Long-Term PDS Development in Research Universities and the Clinicalization of Teacher Education." *Journal of Teacher Education* 48 (March/April 1997): 85-95. a

Bullough, R., et al. "Professional Development Schools: Catalysts for Teacher and School Change." *Teaching and Teacher Education* 13 (February 1997): 153-69. b

Button, K.; Ponticell, J.; and Johnson, M. "Enabling School-University Collaborative Research: Lessons Learned in Professional Development Schools." *Journal of Teacher Education* 47 (January/February 1996): 16-20.

Carnegie Forum on Education and the Economy, Task Force on Teaching as a Profession. *A Nation Prepared: Teachers for the 21st Century.* New York, 1986.

Clark, R. *Professional Development Schools: Policy and Financing, A Guide for Policymakers.* Washington, D.C.: AACTE, 1997.

Clark, R., and Plecki, M. "Professional Development Schools: Their Costs and Financing." In *Making Professional Development Schools Work: Politics, Practices, and Policy,* edited by M. Levine and R. Trachtman. New York: Teachers College Press, 1997.

Darling-Hammond, L., ed. *Professional Development Schools: Schools for Developing a Profession.* New York: Teachers College Press, 1994.

Dewey, J. "The Relation of Theory to Practice in Education." 1904. In *John Dewey on Education: Selected Writings,* edited by R.D. Archambault. Chicago: University of Chicago Press, 1974.

Goodlad, J. *The Dynamics of Educational Change: Toward Responsive Schools. I/D/E/A Reports on Schooling.* New York: McGraw-Hill, 1975.

Goodlad, J. *A Place Called School. Prospects for the Future*. New York: McGraw-Hill, 1984.

Goodlad, J. "School-University Partnerships: Rationale and Concepts." In *School-University Partnerships in Action: Concepts, Cases, and Concerns*, edited by K. Sirotnik, and J. Goodlad. New York: Teachers College Press, 1988.

Goodlad, J. *Teachers for Our Nation's Schools*. San Francisco: Jossey-Bass, 1990.

Goodlad, J. *Educational Renewal: Better Teachers, Better Schools*. San Francisco: Jossey-Bass, 1994.

Grisham, D., et al. "Connecting Communities of Practice Through Professional Development School Activities." *Journal of Teacher Education* 50 (May 1999): 182-91.

Haberman, M. "Twenty-three Reasons Why Universities Can't Educate Teachers." *Journal of Teacher Education* 22 (Summer 1971): 133-40.

Hathaway, W. "Models of School-University Collaboration: National and Local Perspective on Collaborations that Work." Paper presented at the annual meeting of the American Educational Research Association. Chicago, March 1985. ED 253973.

Hausfather, S.; Outlaw, M.; and Strehle, E. "Relationships as a Foundation: Emerging Field Experiences Within Multiple College-School Partnerships." In *Partnerships in Teacher Education: Schools and Colleges Working Together*, edited by T. Warren. Lanham, Md.: University Press of America, 1996.

Hoerr, T.R. "Making Time for Collegiality." *Education Week*, 23 April 1997, pp. 40-44.

Holmes Group. *Tomorrow's Teachers: A Report of the Holmes Group*. East Lansing, Mich., 1986.

Holmes Group. *Tomorrow's Schools: Principles for the Design of Professional Development Schools*. East Lansing, Mich., 1990.

41

Holmes Group. *Tomorrow's Schools of Education*. East Lansing, Mich., 1995.

Levine, M. "Professional Development Schools: More Than a Good Idea." *Teaching and Change* 6, no. 1 (1998): 8-20.

Lieberman, A. "Collaborative Work." *Educational Leadership* 43 no. 5 (1986): 4-8.

Lieberman, A., and Miller, L. *Teachers, Their World and Their Work: Implications for School Improvement*. Alexandria, Va.: Association for Supervision and Curriculum Development, 1984.

Lipsky, M. *Street Level Bureaucracy: Dilemmas of the Individual in Public Services*. New York: Basic Books, 1980.

Miller, L., and Silvernail, D. "Wells Junior High School: Evolution of a Professional Development School." In *Professional Development Schools: Schools for Developing a Profession*, edited by L. Darling-Hammond. New York: Teachers College Press, 1994.

Million, S., and Vare, J. "The Collaborative School." *Phi Delta Kappan* 78 (May 1997): 710-13.

National Council for Accreditation of Teacher Education (NCATE). *Draft Standards for Identifying and Supporting Quality Professional Development Schools*. Washington D.C.: AACTE, 1997.

Neufeld, B. "Professional Practice Schools in Context: New Mixtures of Institutional Authority." In *Professional Practice Schools: Linking Teacher Education and School Reform*, edited by M. Levine. New York: Teachers College Press, 1992.

Parkay, F. "A School/University Partnership that Fosters Inquiry-Oriented Staff Development." *Phi Delta Kappan* 67 (January 1986): 386-89.

Patterson, R.; Michelli, N.; and Pacheco, A. *Centers of Pedagogy: New Structures for Educational Renewal*. San Francisco: Jossey-Bass, 1999.

Peterson, P. *Schools, Groups and Networks: A Political Perspective*. rev. ed. Washington, D.C.: National Education Association, 1977.

Sandholtz, J., and Finan, E. "Blurring the Boundaries to Promote School-University Partnerships." *Journal of Teacher Education* 49 (January/February1998): 13-25.

Sandholtz, J., and Merseth, K. "Collaborating Teachers in a Professional Development School: Inducements and Contributions." *Journal of Teacher Education* 43 (September/October 1992): 308-17.

Sarason, S., et al. *Human Services and Resource Networks*. San Francisco: Jossey-Bass, 1977.

Sirotnik, K., and Goodlad, J., eds. *School-University Partnerships in Action: Concepts, Cases, and Concerns*. New York: Teachers College Press, 1988.

Stallings, J., and Kowalski, T. "Research on Professional Development Schools." In *Handbook of Research on Teacher Education*, edited by W. Houston. New York: Macmillan, 1990.

Sykes, G. "Worthy of the Name: Standards for Professional Development Schools." In *Making Professional Development Schools Work: Politics, Practices, and Policy*, edited by M. Levine and R. Trachtman. New York: Teachers College Press, 1997.

Su, Z. "School-University Partnerships: Ideas and Experiments (1986-90)." Occasional Paper No. 12. Seattle: Institute for the Study of Educational Policy, 1990.

Teitel, L. *Governance: Designing Professional Development School Governance Structures*. Washington, D.C.: AACTE, 1998. a

Teitel, L. "Separations, Divorces, and Open Marriages in Professional Development School Partnerships." *Journal of Teacher Education* 49 (March/April 1998): 85-96. b

Teitel, L. "Review of Research on Professional Development Schools." *ATE Newsletter* 33, no. 1 (1999): 5-7.

Watts, G., and Castle, S. "The Time Dilemma in School Re-structuring." *Phi Delta Kappan* 75 (December 1993): 306-10.

Wise, A. "If We Are Ever Going to 'Professionalize' School Teaching, Universities Must Redesign Education Programs." *The Teacher Educator* 24 (Spring 1989): 29-32.

Wise, A., and Darling-Hammond, L. *Licensing Teachers: Design for a Teaching Profession*. Santa Monica, Calif.: RAND, 1987.

Recent Books Published by the Phi Delta Kappa Educational Foundation

Readings on Leadership in Education
From the Archives of Phi Delta Kappa International
Trade paperback. $22 (PDK members, $16.50)

Profiles of Leadership in Education
Mark F. Goldberg
Trade paperback. $22 (PDK members, $16.50)

Quest for Truth:
Scientific Progress and Religious Beliefs
Mano Singham
Trade paperback. $22 (PDK members, $16.50)

Education in the United Kingdom and Ireland
James E. Green
Trade paperback. $15 (PDK members, $12)

American Education in the 21st Century
Dan H. Wishnietsky
Trade paperback. $22 (PDK members, $16.50)

Use Order Form on Next Page
Or Phone 1-800-766-1156

A processing charge is added to all orders.
Prices are subject to change without notice.

Complete online catalog at http://www.pdkintl.org

Order Form